11-16-07

To community patriot
everywhere !

Sylvia Lovely

New Cities in America

THE LITTLE BLUE BOOK OF BIG IDEAS

How Community Patriots
Can Breathe New Life
Into America's Cities

NEW CITIES IN AMERICA
THE LITTLE BLUE BOOK OF BIG IDEAS

How Community Patriots Can Breathe New Life Into America's Cities

Sylvia L. Lovely

MINERVA PUBLISHING

Published in the USA by
Minerva Publishing
P.O. Box 7311
Louisville, KY 40207

ISBN 0-9760713-0-4

Printed in Canada by Friesens Printers through
Four Colour Imports, Louisville, Kentucky

DEDICATION

To Walter and Alma, my parents, whose inspiration has driven my passion for community building even deeper; and to Bernie, Ross, and David, who drive my future.

–S.L.L.

ACKNOWLEDGMENTS

Writing a book is a lot like community building. It is part inspiration, part sweat equity, and a whole lot of community spirit and hard work. For all these things, I have a number of people to thank, without whom this book would not have been possible.

I begin with Walter and Alma Leach, my parents, whose stories are strewn throughout the book and who served as the chief inspiration for my work in city and community building. I thank Bernie, my husband, and my two boys, Ross and David, who grew up surrounded by local government and community issues. It was at age eight that David turned his face up to me and asked, "Mom, why do you know so many mayors?"

I thank my colleagues at the Kentucky League of Cities and the NewCities Foundation. I thank the KLC board, led by remarkable city officials who toil day in and day out with little pay or recognition. I thank the board of the NewCities Foundation, led by Virginia Fox. I have deep gratitude for her serving as chair, given her distinguished national reputation in public television and education. That she would take time to serve and enhance our vision of public service is a credit to her incredible talent.

I thank Bobbie Bryant, KLC director of communications, for her patience and strong belief in this project, and for her keen intellect that shines through on every page. Thanks to Neil Hackworth, the talented former mayor of Shelbyville, Kentucky, who is known for his pioneering work on downtown revitalization. As KLC's deputy executive director, Neil now puts his abilities to work on the state and national stage. He was instrumental in the completion of this book because of his willingness to shoulder more than his fair share in running the league's day to day operations while this project was ongoing. Likewise, the creative spirit of Bill Hamilton, KLC's deputy director of finance and insurance services, is always a driving force for any major project I undertake.

Tad Long, Robyn Miller, and Steve Austin of the NewCities Foundation staff have taken a fledgling organization and given it life. These folks not only provided day to day advice and written examples of cities practicing the foundation's "Twelve Principles," but also the important moral support that is necessary in a task of this scope.

Thanks go to Diana Taylor, my good friend, and a super talent and public servant in her own right. Her strong editing throughout the process was of invaluable assistance.

Thanks, too, go to Kaye Smith, whose answering of phones exceeds an art form and who played a strong supporting role in proofreading, as did Joseph Coleman. Thanks to Joe Ewalt,

ACKNOWLEDGMENTS

Dag Ryen, and Terri Johnson for their incredible support, written input, and assistance in every way, in this project and others. Also, thanks to members of the Commonwealth Group—Bob Gunnell, Tim Mulloy, Ted Jackson, and Lisa Huber—for their assistance and moral support.

I'm indebted to Bill Thielen, whose strong legal instincts provided the "business sense," allowing me and others to focus on the project's creative aspects.

Special thanks goes to Freda Meriwether, my executive assistant, whose patience and kindness is bottomless and who has crossed the line beyond being an assistant to being a life long friend and helpmate in every way.

Finally, I devote more than one sentence to thanking John McGill. As I grow older, I am more convinced than ever that some encounters with special people are meant to be. That is the case with John and me. I believe that we have formed a working relationship that is meaningful and will last through many more projects such as this. To say he assisted me is inadequate, as it was much more. In editing, re-writing, and bringing others to the cause, he was an essential partner. In addition, he was totally candid, offering invaluable advice on all the questions that arise in a project of this magnitude. I cannot thank him enough for all that he did.

–Sylvia L. Lovely

TABLE OF CONTENTS

INTRODUCTION

The 21st century is unleashing powerful new forces that will affect America and its communities in ways we can only begin to imagine. These forces are global and local, technological and political, known and unknown. Although we can't accurately predict every way that our lives will change, it is clear that we face major challenges in developing communities that can thrive in this exciting but uncertain era.

As this new world of nearly-constant change confronts us, we find ourselves at a critical civic crossroads. A growing number of Americans feel disaffected and disempowered. Civic engagement is declining on the political and social fronts, jeopardizing the health of our democratic process and our ability to build a better future.

It was this reality that gave birth to the NewCities Foundation in February 2001. As executive director and CEO of the Kentucky League of Cities, I had long been involved in the day-to-day operations of cities—helping them deal with everything from legislative issues to insurance coverage to legal advice. It was important work, but it mainly dealt with the "hardware" of a city. What, I began to wonder, about the "software"—the intangibles that make great cities? What about those things in a community that make life more livable and the pursuit of happiness more tangible?

The early days of the foundation's life featured an international conference at Centre College in Danville, Kentucky, that brought experts and visionaries together to discuss what made cities and communities great. We called it "The Morphing of Main Street USA: The Future of America's Heartland Cities."

When we set the date, who could have guessed that our summit would take place only thirteen days after the terrorist attacks on the United States?

As they did virtually every aspect of American life, the events of September 11, 2001, disrupted our conference, particularly since a number of participants were unable to make their flights. But at the same time, the need for a conference on community-building became even more apparent. In the aftermath of 9/11, people wanted connection. Issues of quality of life appeared alongside new concerns over security. This need for community life was, I believe, raised in some respects to a spiritual level. More than ever, all of us seemed to be searching for deeper meaning.

Those who made it to the conference were intent on finding ways to build New Cities. Twelve principles that would help America's heartland cities find ways to thrive in the 21st century were identified. Our vision was given a backbone.

Creating New Cities will not happen, of course, without the hard work and sustained commitment of many people. In the time that has passed since our initial conference, the NewCities Foundation has sought to inform and inspire people throughout America. It is vital that all of us join in a process that can help revitalize American democracy and build communities in which people have a sense of purpose, empowerment, and connection to each other and the world.

We believe people are yearning to feel connected to each other again, to have a basic sense of trust in our systems and in each other. We think such a vision of community—and of great cities—is possible. We think it requires a new kind of person: someone we call a Community Patriot.

In this little blue book, we hope to present ideas that give you the resolve to create a New City and the means to go about it. The payoff will be unprecedented for those who get it right: a quality of life that reflects the progressive vision of citizens who are committed to living in the communities they build.

A resurgence of broad-based citizenship is required

to create and sustain this renaissance. As people gain a greater understanding of the nurturing possibilities of a rich community life, more will return to our smaller cities and towns and, quite probably, more will work to transform our larger cities into a connected collection of neighborhoods and communities.

At the NewCities Foundation inaugural summit, former Abilene, Texas, Mayor Gary McCaleb, director of the Center for Building Community, quoted from a statue in Sydney, Australia: "A city is the greatest work of art possible."

These works of art are only possible with the participation of citizens who understand that we never outgrow our need to come together in community.

We hope this little book will plant some big ideas that help your city. And we trust you will join us in restoring the belief that, together as Community Patriots, we can improve the quality of life for all citizens.

It is time to build a better world.

CHAPTER ONE

THE 21ST CENTURY PATRIOT: COMMUNITY FIRST

September 11, 2001, began as a beautiful day. But even before the horrific news unfolded in New York City, Washington, D.C., and a charred field in Pennsylvania, the day had been bittersweet for me. I was taking my ill mother for a visit to her childhood home in Eastern Kentucky—a place she had had to leave in the early 1950s. It was her first trip in years, and most assuredly it would be her last. I lost my mother at Christmas time that year.

I buckled her into the backseat, slid in under the wheel next to my 81-year-old father, and headed off for what has to be some of the most peaceful countryside on Earth. As we drove through the tiny towns of my parents' upbringing, I watched in the rear view mirror as my mother pressed her face against the glass, taking in the sights for the first time in 50 years, and for the last.

On the way out of West Liberty, a tobacco field in late summer bloom appeared on the right, all golden and glistening. For those whose knowledge about tobacco comes only from the news about its harmful effects, it might be hard to understand the deep meaning the plant has held for generations of Kentucky farmers, particularly those with a small number of acres.

Although its days are numbered as a cash crop, tobacco has sustained small Kentucky towns and small family-owned farms for decades. It gave farmers the means to come to town on Saturdays for "trading," and it connected their children—people such as my father and mother—to the land in an intimate way.

There are not many sights prettier than a field full of ripening tobacco plants on a bright day right before housing—as the harvest is called. The shimmering plants caught our attention, so we stopped the car. My mother was too weak to get out, but my father bounded into the field and posed for my camera, his arms outstretched.

"It's so good to be back in Kentucky!" he called out. I lowered my camera and reminded him that he had been back in Kentucky for 20 years, having returned to the state after being laid off from his job in Ohio. He and my mother had made it as far as Lexington, in the central part of the state, where they took care of my boys while I worked.

"No," he said with conviction. "I'm not in Kentucky 'til I'm in West Liberty."

For me, it was one of those moments of crystal clear understanding. My father knew where home *really* was—and how much it meant. As the terrible events of that day unfolded, I suspect all of us had a yearning for home, for community, for neighbors who would join us in our sorrow and help us through our uncertainty. Community mattered on 9/11 and in the days that followed. But for my parents, community had always mattered. It had defined them. It had truly been home. My father had expressed an attachment that was as old as time.

We would experience a cataclysmic clash of two worlds on that day. When the airplanes crashed into the World Trade Center towers, into the Pentagon, and into that Pennsylvania field, America was in many ways changed forever. The world was upon us with an impact that few had imagined—a world fueled by something dark and ugly. Despite the horror, in many ways that day also launched a worthy quest in America: a pursuit of lives that are more satisfying, warm, and nurturing, a desire to join in community. It underscored the need to re-establish the connection that my father's feelings about West Liberty suggested were so necessary for our sense of completeness.

It is unfortunately true that as the days and months passed, we saw that quest almost disappear. We settled into the reality of homeland security and airport searches and TV images of bombings and atrocities, and too often we looked for ways to numb ourselves to it all. One respondent to a network news poll probably put it best: "We watch back-to-back reality TV shows just to escape the real reality."

That statement probably reflects the attitude that many of us hold—possibly because we don't believe we can make much of a difference anymore. We had a chance to build on a spirit of neighborly concern and compassion in the immediate aftermath of 9/11, but we failed to do so. And I think we are yearning, still, to find a way to regain a sense of community, to feel as profoundly connected as my father did standing in that tobacco field near West Liberty, joyful that he was finally, truly home.

I am convinced that all of us can still find home. This book is about hope. Although it doesn't claim to have all the answers, it sets out ways that we as individuals can come together to create the cities and communities that bring out the best in us.

This book is also a call for a new kind of citizen—someone who understands small-town values but realizes that communities can no longer stand in isolation from the larger world. It is what the NewCities Foundation is all about, to create New Cities based on the commitment and good works of new citizens.

We call this new citizen the Community Patriot.

A new form of patriotism is at the center of this movement. This is not just about flag-waving, crowd-cheering patriotism. And it certainly isn't about political finger pointing that tries to use patriotism as a form of one-upmanship. Rather, it is about patriotism that is thoughtful, serious, and willing to question the status quo.

That willingness must include self-criticism and the ability to correct a bad decision or a policy that isn't working. This, of course, involves a good measure of courage in an era where partisan shouting and derision too often pass for legitimate debate and reasoned assessment.

There is reason enough to believe that candor is precisely what people want in their leaders. Adlai Stevenson put it best. When he accepted the nomination to run for president at the Democratic convention in 1952, he said: "Where we have erred, let there be not denial. Where we have wronged the public trust, let there be no excuses. Self-criticism is the secret weapon of democracy, and candor and confession are good for the political soul."

How refreshing it would be to hear that kind of honesty from leaders today—at the local, state, and federal levels. By creating a climate that welcomes frank assessment and open debate for the good of all, we can move toward putting this secret weapon to work for us again.

Community Patriotism brings people together to address special concerns—people who share the same selflessness that our ancestors exhibited in building this nation. Community Patriots are men and women willing to put others first—willing to step out of their comfort zones and take an active role in promoting, protecting, and providing for their communities.

Combining the best of a strong sense of local identity with the opportunities that the world and its global marketplace offer, the Community Patriot works to strengthen his city's "livability" quotient while also helping position it to survive and thrive in the global arena.

The Community Patriot understands that we are in an era of technological advance unprecedented in human history for its rapid change and constant challenge. But even so, the challenge is in many ways similar to what my parents faced. When they had to leave Eastern Kentucky to find work, it must have been a fearsome decision to uproot their young family. Had they not had a car, a road outside their house, knowledge about a place called Dayton, and a fair amount of gumption, my parents probably would have stayed in the Appalachian hills—probably without work.

What is different today is that our options for choosing where to live and work are seemingly endless. We can look beyond our immediate circumstances to make our mark, but our heads are often turned by what is "out there." We crane our necks to see celebrities in restaurants or walking a red carpet at the Academy Awards, but rarely look to that which is right at our fingertips.

We fail to recognize that our individual involvement in our communities can shape our lives in a very real way. And it can hold the key to our fulfillment.

One goal of this book is to define community work in a way that makes it an achievable goal for Community Patriots. Much of what we hear about citizenship has been gauzy, light and high above the fray. Because we have long focused on platitudes but not paid enough attention to practical tactics at the local and individual levels, a dynamic idea of citizenship and its true meaning has not been able to take root, much less blossom.

When the NewCities Foundation came up with a series of Twelve Principles for Ongoing Success—its "dynamic dozen"—it did so with the idea of providing concrete ways for Community Patriots to create New Cities and thriving communities.

A 21st century Community Patriot is a person who grasps the full impact of the changes we are facing, takes charge to help make his or her community a great one, and sees how that community must fit into the broader global picture to succeed.

New Cities, in short, allow citizens to live good and satisfying lives with personal connections to each other while taking advantage of what the world "out there" has to offer.

Why "city?" We have purposely called these principles of city building because cities are at the heart of the American experiment and the American dream.

The gathering of people in city life has been with us for centuries. Even in the rugged days of the frontier American West where individualism was prized, cowhands gathered in saloons to share tales of lonely nights and high noon adventure on the plains.

Today there are more than 19,000 cities in the United States. They range in size from New York City and Los Angeles to Frenchburg, Kentucky, and Madison, Indiana. All have a common thread. People have come together to share their lives and develop opportunities for economic prosperity, culture, education, commerce, religion, and the other hallmarks of personal fulfillment.

Cities are the heart and center of community, and if the center holds, so does the community.

Community Patriots go about building New Cities with three key steps: by learning the fundamentals of city building, by discovering how to participate in every phase of civic engagement, and by acting to create great communities with strong cities at the center.

The foundation for it all rests with the Twelve Principles for Ongoing Success.

CHAPTER TWO

WHAT A COMMUNITY PATRIOT NEEDS TO KNOW

Even in the midst of tumultuous change, it is the things that never change that are often the most striking.

Near the end of her life, my mother loved nothing more than to walk through her favorite Wal-Mart—not exactly my idea of fun. Usually I refused to shop there, but with my mother having precious little to enjoy and precious little time left, I accompanied her every Saturday morning on her three-hour visit to the store. It was a labor of love for me, and I relished the enjoyment she got out of each trip.

She would lean against her cart (out of necessity as her strength waned) while gazing at the myriad colors around her and touching all in her path—little girls' velvet dresses, packages of candy, knit caps… anything and everything.

It is something I treasure about her—the ability she had

to find fascination in so many things that I (and perhaps you) take for granted. When her life was nearing its end, her hospice doctor wanted to adjust her medications to allow her to do the things she most enjoyed. He asked what that would be. "I like the little things," she said.

That memory still humbles me. My life is typical of many. We go, go, go as hard as we can, and we seek to live a fast and exciting life. I was always on the run to meet important people and do the big, important things. But my mother's illness changed that. I came to see that life really is comprised of the little things that we do every day and that it's those little things—the things that make real connections with others—that supply much of our joy.

I believe everybody has their moment of truth, when the idea of stopping to smell the roses is no longer just a cliché to dismiss. Instead, it becomes a call to make a choice about how we *really* want to live.

I believe most of us feel there is something missing—and I believe that is largely because we no longer feel connected to our neighborhoods, or communities, or cities, or even our country. We want not only to appreciate the little things, but also to share them. We want to feel we belong. We want to believe that we can make a difference.

And so, I think every Community Patriot needs to know that revitalizing a city isn't just about getting involved politically or taking charge of a program that will benefit the community. It's about committing to a sense of togetherness and neighborly concern that, ultimately, is the driving force behind any civilized system—of government or living.

Once you commit to concern for others as well as yourself and your family, the next steps are easier. You talk to people and find out what is important to them. And you listen—closely. That is the critical element, I think, the ability to relate. You have to have a strong connection to the place you live and to the people living around you—all kinds of people, from every corner of the community.

In all my years of community building, what I've learned is that the basics never really change. What has changed is the way we live our lives. While the fundamentals are the same, how we use them to achieve our goals is dramatically different.

New Cities of the 21st century have a common denominator. They do particular things extraordinarily well. They provide strong connections within the community and to the larger, outside world. They promote civic pride in both physical place and spirit. And, of course, they provide economic opportunities for their citizens—something no city can succeed without.

To achieve the status of a great community, Community Patriots can rely on the "dynamic dozen" set of guidelines established by the NewCities Foundation. These Twelve Principles for Ongoing Success are at the heart of the mission. They are:

- Connect to the world
- Cultivate leadership and civic involvement
- Embrace healthy living
- Encourage youth, diversity, and inclusiveness
- Feed the mind and nurture the soul
- Remain true to the city's uniqueness
- Don't merely grow … plan and develop over time
- Build beautifully and steward the environment
- Recruit, retain and generate wealth
- Overcome obstacles
- Rethink boundaries
- Buy locally, sell globally

Fortunately, there are already many examples of cities and citizens putting these principles into action. Let's take a closer look at each principle and see how communities—large and small—are using the principles to achieve promising results.

Connect to the World

"The day is coming, and it ain't going to be long, when you ain't even gonna have to leave your living room. No more schools, no more bodegas, no more tabernacles, no more cineplexes. You're going to snuggle up to your fiber optics, baby, and bliss out."

Diane Frolov and Andrew Schneider (*Northern Exposure: Heal Thyself*, 1993)

In a cockeyed sort of way, there's wisdom to be found in this backhanded ode to technology. While there's underlying sarcasm here (technology as a tool to avoid face-to-face interaction with people and the world), the fact is that tech breakthroughs are giving people and communities the chance to connect on a global scale.

This is a time for broadening horizons—both economically and socially. Communities must look for ways to thrive in global markets, and citizens must embrace new cultures and new residents who represent a myriad of cultural and geographical backgrounds.

The Principle in Action

Going Seriously International: Fort Worth, Texas

Until a few years ago, attitudes about the global economy in Fort Worth, Texas, were similar to what you'd find in most larger American cities. City leaders appreciated jobs created by foreign investors but decried job losses to low-wage countries. They acknowledged long-standing cultural ties with other countries, but did little to promote them. They supported educational exchanges with sister cities, but invested only modestly in international programs.

All that changed in the 1990s as Fort Worth felt the pinch of a declining oil industry, low prices on agricultural products, and the closure of a nearby Air Force base. After some soul-searching, the city decided it needed to increase its efforts to strengthen international trade and goodwill exchanges.

In 1997 the city authorized creation of a full-fledged international center that consolidated the efforts of several independent organizations. The city leased an office building and offered space to the Small Business Administration, the economic development office the neighboring Mexican state of Chiapas, the Asian-American Business Council of Tarrant County, the local Sister Cities Commission, the

Chamber of Commerce, and others.

The initiative worked well for a while, but city leaders soon realized that sharing a location wasn't the entire answer. At the beginning of the new century, the center began to place more emphasis on trade and economic development.

According to center director Sigi Frias, the city ultimately recognized that it takes business-savvy people to promote job creation and commercial investment. The international center intensified its cooperation with the Fort Worth Chamber of Commerce and became immersed in developing a detailed business strategy.

The realignment is already producing results. A French manufacturer of paragliders plans to construct a facility in Fort Worth that will create 25 to 30 high-skilled jobs, and a Canadian manufacturer has already opened a plant that at full capacity will add 40 jobs. Both companies worked closely with the international center's staff, using free office space while considering their location decisions.

Frias and his staff understand that the global marketplace is constantly changing. The era of recruiting large-scale foreign investment may be over, but smaller manufacturers don't demand the kind of tax incentives or infrastructure investments that a Toyota or BMW plant would. Local leaders have become far more conscious of tracking the net benefit to the community from any such recruitment or trade promotion.

"The primary thing is that you can't have an operation that focuses on trade and not measure your success in dollars," Frias says. "It's almost too simple to point out, but it's a critical benchmark."

Projects shepherded by the center bring more than $1 million annually to the local economy, a return far greater than what the city invests in staff and overhead. The center also reinforces the city's image as an international trade leader by conducting seminars, trade missions, and leadership exchanges. Each summer the mayor convenes a trade summit and an awards luncheon that attract business leaders and mayors from surrounding communities.

The Fort Worth experience underscores the importance not only of recognizing the impact of the global marketplace, but of thinking strategically when defining a city's role in that market.

High Tech Rescues the Steeple People: Campbellsville, Kentucky

What do the ringing of church bells and microwave Internet connections have in common? Well, Campbellsville, Kentucky, is a leader in both, and both are important to the city's connection to the world economy. The problem was, once upon a time the connection was nearly severed.

The story begins with a work-study program at

Campbellsville College, where students were offered an opportunity to build lecterns, pews, and other church items to earn money toward their tuition at the traditionally Baptist school. One day a church approached the shop manager and asked if he and his students could build a steeple. The result was a lightweight but structurally strong aluminum design. Before long, it became a tremendous commercial success.

The steeple company that eventually was created, Campbellsville Industries, is now in private hands and is briskly shipping its product to clients across the United States. But a couple of years ago, the owners considered relocating because there was no high-speed Internet capability in rural Campbellsville, which has a population of just over 10,000.

The local phone company was unwilling to provide such service, and the local cable operator was unable to. So city leaders, with the help of the Kentucky League of Cities, went searching for a solution. The answer was wireless Internet access. Today, a wireless broadband hub attached to city hall offers high-speed connections to the steeple manufacturer and dozens of other local businesses, enabling them to do instant messaging to clients around the country and around the world.

High-speed Internet access is a must for doing business in today's marketplace. It allows companies to compete anywhere and everywhere.

"Before broadband, we were connected at 56K; basically, it creeped," says Campbellsville Industries spokesperson Roger Moran. "Now we don't see any need to go anyplace else. We've got the speed, efficiency, and manpower here to get the product out the door."

As a result, church bells in a half-dozen countries ring out of Campbellsville steeples. And more are on the way.

Learning to Love the E-Village: Blacksburg, Virginia

The city with the highest per capita use of the Internet is neither in Silicon Valley nor in some high tech Asian center. It's Blacksburg, Virginia, home of the innovative communications network, the Blacksburg Electronic Village.

Blacksburg, a town of about 40,000 situated in the scenic New River Valley on the western slopes of the Blue Ridge Mountains, languished in relative anonymity through most of the 20th century. It served as a mercantile center for the local farming community and as home to Virginia Tech University, which gradually became the town's largest employer and dominant force.

By the early 1990s, Virginia Tech had also become a major research institution with 25,000 undergraduates and a rapidly increasing number of graduate students in the sciences and high-tech engineering. As these students spread throughout the community, the university faced a major communications challenge: how to keep everyone connected.

The innovative answer was the Blacksburg Electronic Village, a hard-wired network covering the entire town, constructed in partnership with town officials and the local phone company. It took more than two years to install digital switching equipment and fiber backbone along every street, road, and alley. Then project managers spent two years testing software packages that included Internet services.

The result is a system that makes service available from a variety of private sector providers as a standard amenity. Today more than 87 percent of Blacksburg residents are Internet users, and more than 75 percent of the city's businesses use it for marketing and client communications.

The benefits extend far beyond the university and the private sector. The network provides discussion groups (via message boards) on public policy, more efficient communication between citizens and town officials, and greater visibility for community events. Indeed, the electronic village reaches into almost every aspect of local life, making the citizens of Blacksburg among the world's best connected.

Cultivate Leadership and Civic Involvement

"Leadership is solving problems. The day soldiers stop bringing you their problems is the day you have stopped leading them. They have either lost confidence that you can help or concluded you do not care. Either case is a failure of leadership."

Colin Powell, from *Leadership Secrets of Colin Powell*

In many cases, disheartened citizens have the same feeling about leadership in government. They've concluded that government either can't help or doesn't care.

This suggests a growing crisis in the health of our democratic process—as reflected in the voting statistics and the myriad ways in which people don't seem to be involved as much as they once were in community and civic affairs.

Cities can play a fundamental role in restoring faith in government—because leadership at the local level involves a more direct connection between government officials and the public they serve.

By getting people involved and demonstrating that they can make a difference, the level of civic engagement is enhanced and, in turn, the demand for quality leadership is increased. New citizens recognize the power they have to determine their quality of life—and can begin to hold officials accountable. It's also the way to bring new thinking and new people into both the political process and positions of leadership.

The Principle in Action

How One Person Helped a Community Find Itself: Bayview, Virginia

Tucked in the middle of farmland on Virginia's eastern shore, Bayview in the mid-1990s was a small rural community whose residents lived mostly in dilapidated one-room shacks that had no running water, no central air, and no indoor plumbing. It seemed an ideal place—or target, depending on your point of view—for the state of Virginia to build a maximum security prison.

That's when Alice Coles took matters into her own hands and helped a community realize its power to shape its own destiny. She led the fight against the prison, which was proposed in 1995, and won. But the story doesn't end there. Out of this effort came the Bayview Citizens for Social Justice (BCSJ), which Coles co-founded.

Buoyed by their victory over the prison issue, Coles and a growing number of people began to dream about improving their quality of life. The dream turned into a plan to acquire the skills and gather the resources necessary to purchase land to build clean, functional housing.

It took persistence and a fair amount of salesmanship to raise that money—and an engaged citizenry to raze the dilapidated shacks they once called home. Today, more than

60 families have relocated across the street from the site of their former residences into new, subsidized housing.

The new houses have front porches, which is something Coles and others had to persuade highly reluctant state and federal funding agencies to approve. Whatever the condition of the old houses, their porches had served as a focal point of family life, a place where stories were passed down from generation to generation, where Bible passages were recited, and where lessons in life were taught. And they were places where neighbors gathered.

Alice Coles understood what the state and federal governments did not: this was about community. This went to the heart of things. It took enormous persistence, but Coles and others were finally able to convince the agencies to include porches.

Alice Coles is now Bayview's executive director. But long before her title, she had shown how one person can make a difference—and convince others that they can, too.

Bringing City Hall to the Neighborhood: Boulder, Colorado

In an age where communication is key, Boulder, Colorado, decided not to wait for its citizens to get in touch, but to actively seek their feedback. In 2001 the city created the

Neighborhood Association Contact Team, a group of city employees recruited to serve as liaisons between the city and neighborhood associations.

Team members attend monthly meetings of neighborhood associations, share city programs and services announcements, and take notes about neighborhood concerns and events. The city representatives also attend a contact team meeting each month to share information about the neighborhoods and to learn about city programs and services.

This team approach allows the neighborhood services coordinator to learn about issues in a timely manner and to respond immediately to any requests for assistance. City workers participating as members of the contact team are typically assigned to the neighborhood where they live and are paid up to $100 for each monthly association meeting attended.

By taking the lead on opening the lines of communication, the program goes a long way in encouraging citizen participation in local government and the community.

Transforming a Sour Situation into Tupelo Honey: Tupelo, Mississippi

Haven Acres in Tupelo, Mississippi, was a scary place to live a decade ago. This predominantly African-American, low-income neighborhood was riddled with crime, youth gangs, prostitution, and drug houses. Even the police were afraid to respond to calls without backup. But all that began to change in the late 1990s. Long-time residents decided they needed to take back their neighborhood.

The Haven Acres Neighborhood Association was created in 1998. Residents banded together with city officials and police to institute a zero tolerance policy for crime. Within 24 months, neighborhood crime was reduced by 86 percent.

Led by President Mattie Mabry, the neighborhood association also raised more than $100,000 to buy land and start building a $1.1 million community center. The center is now home to a thriving Boys and Girls Club that offers an encouraging alternative to gang life. In 2003 the community center served more than 260 kids each day during the summer.

The Haven Acres story is one of hope and possibilities. It shows what strong, civic minded individuals can accomplish when they come together to take on a problem that once seemed impossible to overcome.

Embrace Healthy Living

"The health of the people is really the foundation upon which all their happiness and all their powers as a state depend."

Benjamin Disraeli, speech in the House of Commons, 1877

Whether it is enacting a smoking ban in public places or building extensive bike paths for commuting to work or recreation, finding ways to encourage healthy living is critical to having a strong community.

New Cities also recognize that emotional health is equally important and can, in fact, be a major factor in preventing physical problems. Communities that offer programs such as tai chi or yoga and businesses that are attuned to stress-reducing practices such as flex time are more productive.

The Principle in Action

Baby, You Can Drive My Car (or Not): Liverpool, England

John, Paul, George, and Ringo (the Beatles, for those of you of a younger generation) would be proud of how their hometown has come up with a brilliant connection to improve health by improving the transportation system.

It might seem a long and winding road (I promise that's the last Beatles song reference) to connect public transportation with health care, but some pretty insightful researchers discovered otherwise. The effects of personal mobility on the well-being of the community became a well-studied priority.

"Transport poverty" was identified as a real problem for a growing number of people within the working class city of Liverpool and the surrounding Merseyside region of 1.4 million people. With Merseyside's household car access level at around 60 percent—lower than the national average—public transportation is vital.

A 1996 study found that the number of trips people made to and from home was directly related to their income. It concluded that people with the lowest incomes experience what was termed "social exclusion" because they don't have affordable transportation—resulting in overall poor health, anxiety, stress, and depression. These factors ultimately contribute to increased mortality.

The study also linked inadequate public transportation to depriving citizens of training and employment opportunities and limiting personal lifestyle access to stores with affordable healthy foods, emergency services, and leisure and social activities.

Merseyside decided to act.

Liverpool and the region's four other cities collaborated with Merseytravel, the bus transport company, to develop a transport plan that included a section dedicated to "improving the quality of life of children, young people, families at risk, and older people." Service to disabled individuals was also a focus. Throughout the planning, people were encouraged to provide input.

Launched in 2000, the plan dedicated more than $400 million of funding from various governments, nonprofit organizations and private sources over a multi-year period. To date, the plan has achieved nearly 70 percent of its performance goals. The number of Merseyside residents who live within ten minutes of a bus is now at 90 percent.

For those who don't rely on public transportation or drive cars, the Merseyside plan also focuses on cycling and walking. Programs to encourage cycling have increased the number of people who bike to work. And the initiative has spawned a number of other programs as well, including:

- The "Scooter Commuter" program, which encourages people living in out-of-the-way areas to commute to a bus or to work via scooter. The city of St. Helens in Merseyside identified 50 people who had serious obstacles to obtaining work, bought 50 scooters, and trained the people how to rent and use them safely. All 50 have found jobs and can choose to open an option to buy savings accounts to purchase the scooters.

- Merseyside's Child Pedestrian Safety Training program, which focuses on teaching safe pedestrian skills to children ages 5-7 in certain low-income areas. Local schools and volunteers pitch in.
- A partnership between schools in the Park Brow area and the bus line to transport children from home to school and back. Called the Park Brow Breakfast Club, the bus also provides breakfast for the children.

The Merseyside Transport Plan has had a dramatic impact on the environment and has helped meet planning and zoning challenges throughout the five-city region. But most important, it has made life safer and healthier—both physically and emotionally—for people from all walks of life, particularly those at risk.

John Lennon once asked us to imagine. Liverpool and Merseyside took him up on it.

They've Got a Peaceful, Easy Feeling: Bismarck, North Dakota

In Bismarck, the capital of North Dakota, people have a robust approach to life. Their summers are short and their winters are wicked, and the combination seems to make them unusually resilient. Rather than yield passively to the confining nature of harsh winters, they embrace sports, recreation, and outdoor activities to actively make the best of the situation. This approach is also the likely result of a farming culture and nature-focused heritage.

"We certainly take advantage of good weather whenever we get it," said Becky Jones Mahlum, the city's public information officer, "but we thrive in the cold weather, too—from kids to older folks. I think it's just part of a being a North Dakotan, with our history as farmers and outdoorsmen. We're kind of tough."

In 2004 Bismarck was named the least stressful city in America (among small metro areas) by *Sperling's Best Places*, which ranks cities on numerous trends and livability factors. Over a recent twelve month period, Bismarck also was chosen one of the nation's ten safest metro areas and one of the best places to locate a small business.

Bismarck's 57,000 residents have lots of options for sports. Named a 2004 "Sportstown" by *Sports Illustrated*, Bismarck has semi-pro teams, including the Bismarck Bobcats in hockey and the Dakota Wizards of the Continental Basketball Association.

But they don't just watch. Bismarck has more than 35 parks and gardens, 30 miles of hiking trails, and five ice skating rinks, as well as dozens of fitness centers, golf courses, and skiing venues. Summer sports, karate classes, and camping programs are maintained through its parks and recreation department. Year round, people of all ages get out and go. There are a series of programs, including such obscure sports as curling, serving senior citizens.

The healthy lifestyle isn't just fun and games. The city works with neighboring communities to provide a strong public health service that focuses on prevention and outreach for at-risk populations.

The health department provides such programs as home health visits for families and babies, weekly well-baby and children's clinics, tobacco control and smoking cessation programs, and the Women's Way program that provides free breast and cervical cancer screenings to eligible residents. Bismarck celebrates such events as "Drinking Water Week" and provides school nurses, fast becoming a luxury in many school systems nationwide.

One new program, the Dental Gap Clinic, serves the area's uninsured and under insured residents. The Bismarck-Burleigh Health Department works with several partners to provide access to basic and urgent dental care for individuals living at or below 200 percent of the federal poverty level. Launched in 2004, the clinic is expected to serve 2,400 people the first year.

An active job market also keeps the stress level low. With

a highly educated workforce, Bismarck has good jobs and an unemployment rate that has ranged between two and three percent for the last ten years. Eighty-three percent of public high school graduating seniors go to college. The average length of stay on the job is just over eight years and the turnover rate is less than ten percent.

With steady and satisfying work, health outreach to those who can't afford it, preventive measures, a wonderful zoo, and the great outdoors with lots of activities beckoning, it is clear that, in Bismarck, fitness is a priority.

If There's a Norse God of Biking, He Lives in Cycle City: Odense, Denmark

Named after Odin, the Norse god of war, poetry, and wisdom, the city of Odense dates to pre-Viking times. It is Denmark's third-largest city. And while it is steeped in history (it is the home of Hans Christian Andersen), it also happens to be home to some of the fastest people on two wheels—and a *lot* of them.

During the 1990s Odense witnessed an increase in bicycle usage with approximately 50 percent of its residents deciding to ride. Recognizing how cycling improved vehicular traffic and offered other benefits, such as improving ecology and health, Odense started its "Cycle City" project in 1999 with the goal of increasing the number of cyclists and their safety.

The city began by focusing funds not only on continued expansion of the infrastructure, but also on such issues as rights, accessibility, service, fun experiences, maintenance, and quality. To engage more people, city leaders marketed biking as a lifestyle choice for families, seniors, and working professionals. Many of the campaigns are directed toward children and young people—based on the belief that it is easier to establish good traffic habits than to change bad ones.

Odense Cycle City, as the town often calls itself, includes Odense Central Station, an underground bike parking lot that has video surveillance, music, special locking arrangements, a water fountain, baggage lockers, and showcases for bicycle equipment. On the city's website, project manager and civil engineer Troels Andersen is understandably proud when he writes: "This parking lot expresses a standard that even the finest car parking lots can hardly live up to." He also notes, "By choosing the highest quality in all solutions for cyclists, we can persuade a lot more people to start."

The city's persuasiveness includes things like the "green wave" running light system, located on sidewalks a few feet away from traffic lights. The staggered lights alert cyclists when stoplights are about to change, and the system is based on the standard speed of cycling instead of that of cars.

Nationally, Denmark sponsors an annual "Bike to Work" month each spring, and Odense has exceeded 9,000 participants. Danes cycle an average of three kilometers every day. But even in a bicycle nation, Odense is kilometers (not to mention miles) ahead of the pack.

Encourage Youth, Diversity, and Inclusiveness

"I see no hope for the future of our people if they are dependent on the frivolous youth of today, for certainly all youth are reckless beyond words. When I was a boy, we were taught to be discreet and respectful of elders, but the present youth are exceedingly wise and impatient of restraint."

Hesiod, 8th century B.C.

It's easy to be wary of youth. In fact, it's pretty much a tradition—especially when you consider that Hesiod, a Greek poet, was fussing about them around 740 B.C. in much the same way we gripe about kids today.

But the development of New Cities hinges on the involvement of youth. Our younger people need to be encouraged and included in the planning, execution, and implementation of community initiatives. Channeled properly, youthful enthusiasm and insight produce imaginative solutions and energetic contributions.

Diversity and inclusiveness are equally important goals. As we become more and more of a culturally and racially diverse society, it is vital that everyone feel a part of the system if democracy is to function effectively and justly.

The Principle in Action

Thinking Out of the Box(es): Lakewood, Colorado

It was the city that third- and fourth-graders built. Box City, that is. In Lakewood, Colorado, the community planning and development department partnered with a local elementary school to teach students what is involved in planning and developing a community. To do it, they let kids take cardboard boxes and build an entire city.

Lakewood is just one of many cities that participate each year in this national program created by the Center for Understanding the Built Environment (CUBE). Box City promotes an understanding of historic preservation and urban design by combining art and architecture, creative thinking, city planning, design and construction, fun, and learning into one hands-on comprehensive educational experience. Kids use various size boxes, developing their own town in the process.

Through the program, Lakewood city officials spend several months teaching students city planning concepts, including land-use planning, environmental issues, and community infrastructure needs. Children also participate in scavenger hunts to gather specific items in the community, neighborhood walks to learn about and explore the city's infrastructure, and sessions with local police officers to learn about citizenship and community safety.

All of this culminates in the main event, the building of Box City. The half-day exercise challenges students to apply their new knowledge to create a city by working in teams to build just about every structure a city might have. They also have to choose the ideal locations for their buildings.

By the end of the process, students have not only built an entire city, they also have come to recognize how many connections there are between both buildings and areas of a community. By seeing the need for a pleasing whole, the students begin to appreciate what really makes a well-planned city.

When Being Number One Was Something to Shun: Fort Myers, Florida

In 1997 Fort Myers, Florida was named the most segregated community in the South by *Population Today* magazine. Just days after the announcement of that dubious distinction, a group of concerned citizens formed Lee County Pulling Together (LCPT) to explore what the community could do to reduce racial division.

Calling on eight community leaders with diverse backgrounds to serve on a steering committee and gathering approximately 40 volunteers of mixed race to serve on a working council, LCPT began to engage the community's citizens in small group dialogues on race relations.

The discussion groups attracted more than 600 participants in the first two years and resulted in several ideas for breaking down racial barriers. From creating a multiracial community choir and fielding a racially diverse baseball team to enhancing the community with a park for underprivileged children and helping build a Habitat for Humanity home, the community changed course and continues to make progress.

Breaking Down the Barriers: Clearwater, Florida

In response to the growing Hispanic population in Clearwater, Florida, the city's police department has taken a proactive role in building bridges with the Hispanic community. Barriers created by cultural differences and language are being addressed through several innovative programs developed with input from an inter-departmental Hispanic task force and community leaders.

The Overtime Translation Program and the Spanish Interpretation Program allow off-duty bilingual officers and trained civilians to assist at crime and accident scenes as needed. Members of the Hispanic business community and civic leaders hold periodic focus groups to promote dialogue with the police department and allow citizens to effectively communicate their needs and concerns.

In addition, through grants and other funding, the Tampa Bay/City of Clearwater YWCA Hispanic Outreach Center was opened in November 2002, providing bilingual childcare, advocacy and interpreter services, a training facility, health and nutrition services, and language classes. The facility also serves as the offices for the Mexican Consulate and the government of the state of Hidalgo, Mexico, which is the native home of many of Clearwater's immigrants.

Through all of these efforts, the police department has demonstrated its commitment to reaching out. By learning the language and becoming familiar with the Hispanic culture (including sending some officers to Mexico for direct interaction), the police department has been better able to build trust and respect within the Hispanic community. Now, both groups are seeing progress toward a more inclusive city.

The efforts have not gone unnoticed. Clearwater's police department received the 2003 Program Excellence Award from the International City/County Management Association (ICMA) for its Operation Apoyo Hispano outreach program. It also has been cited as a model police community outreach program by the Police Professionalism Initiative of the University of Nebraska.

Feed the Mind and Nurture the Soul

"He who rejects change is the architect of decay. The only human institution that rejects progress is the cemetery."

Harold Wilson, from *Baron of Rievaulx*

Because change keeps coming at us at a speed never before witnessed, adapting to it requires a commitment to lifelong learning. Progress, so to speak, happens. Those communities that fail to encourage ongoing learning may well start to resemble cemeteries.

Because technology is leapfrogging so quickly, it is virtually impossible to predict what kind of jobs will be available in ten years—or perhaps even five. What can be predicted with reasonable certainty is that people who are open to learning will adapt more quickly and successfully. The same can be said for a city.

Lest we become 21st century automatons, gearing our minds only to fill a job requirement, it is equally critical that a community emphasize its cultural gifts and enhance what it has to offer. Jobs may sustain our lives, but it is through the arts and education that we experience life on a broader, even spiritual, plane.

I recall when a group of my associates visited Stowe, Vermont, the home of the von Trapp family of *The Sound of Music* fame after they left Austria. The Trapp Family Lodge is a popular visitors' destination, and the resort area includes horse-drawn carriage rides.

One of our group said he was amazed when the person driving the carriage began to quote Shakespeare and make any number of other references that suggested he was far more intellectual and well read than you'd expect a tourists' carriage driver to be. It turns out that the driver was a former English professor.

Why, my friend wanted to know, had this man wound up in a small Vermont community giving carriage rides? Because he loved the place and the people, the driver said. Besides, it wasn't as if he couldn't continue to read and learn—and his work allowed him to meet interesting people and have stimulating conversations.

Such is the kind of community we should strive to build—where the emphasis isn't just on "learning" to get through school or gain a degree, but where education remains a lifelong process of discovery and wonder. It's through such exploration that the soul is enriched. A New City strives to create the kind of climate that encourages people in this regard.

The Principle in Action

Short on Enrollment but Long on Vision: Cloverport, Kentucky

There are only about 1,200 people in the town and just 320 students in grades K through 12, but Cloverport, Kentucky, nevertheless offers an educational experience that is remarkable for its innovation and farsightedness.

At Frederick Fraize High School in Cloverport, a program called Discover College allows students to earn an associate degree by the time they graduate from high school—thus enabling them to obtain a degree without paying college tuition.

"Basically, I wanted to redefine the senior year of high school for our students," says Dr. J.B. Skaggs, superintendent of the Cloverport Independent School District. "Essentially we're giving our students employment skills along with a great education."

The school district forged a partnership with nearby Owensboro Community and Technical College that allows students to attend OCTC at no cost. The program is sustained through contributions and fundraising activities—which underscores the commitment of the entire community, from parents to teachers to citizens in general.

Skaggs established a strategy that emphasizes studies in the core curriculum in the lower grades—thus allowing juniors and seniors the chance to take dual credit courses that count toward a high school diploma and college credit. As a result, a high school senior can earn up to 30 college hours.

The school district also lets students attend a vocational school in neighboring Hardinsburg, and is developing another partnership with the Owensboro Vocational School for students who opt not to attend college. In these cases, too, there is no cost to the student.

"We know that most of our students will leave Cloverport when they graduate, but we want to give them every reason to come back to their hometown at some point in their lives," Skaggs says. "In our hearts, this is a thriving community. We know our vision of the future, and we're here to stay."

When Art Becomes a Town:
Laren, Netherlands

Nestled in the Dutch countryside about a half hour drive from Amsterdam is the quaint little town of Laren, which continues to tie its reputation and livelihood to art and the creative process.

Laren was the home of several impressionist and expressionist painters, including prominent members of the so-called Hague school as well as American artist William Henry Singer, Jr., heir to a Pittsburgh steel fortune. After his death, Singer's wife founded the Singer Museum in Laren, a focal point for the Dutch art world.

Laren's picturesque setting, with canals, tree-lined bike paths, swan-inhabited ponds, and massive oaks (Holland's champion oak sits on a farm just outside the city), continues to draw both artists and tourists. On weekends in late spring and early summer, painters from throughout Europe flock to the Brink, the shady central park in the old city, and set up their easels in an open-air exhibition that rivals the famous *Place du Tertre* in Paris. The art show draws thousands of tourists, who have made the town's hostels and restaurants among the most sought-out and commercially successful in Northern Europe.

Laren's artistic inclination doesn't end with painting. The city has also become famous for its music. The summer jazz festival features some of the most prominent jazz artists in the world. The city also hosts several folk dancing exhibitions and troupe competitions. Laren is a classic example of a community that has built on its strengths, its natural beauty and the work of artists who have captured it on canvas and in music.

Turning Skid Row Into Artful Living: Grand Rapids, Michigan

In Grand Rapids, Michigan, some visionaries are working hard to transform blighted downtown areas into invitingly artful areas—in one case, quite literally. Developers have begun a $7.5 million renovation program known as the Avenue for the Arts Initiative, which aims initially to transform four vacant and rundown buildings into 23 loft apartments designed with amenities that will be attractive to artists at an affordable rent. Plans also include studio space, a gallery, a café, and other retail space.

"You'd almost have to live in this community to fully appreciate what's being done, in particular on Division Avenue," says Andy Guy of the Michigan Land Institute and a resident of Grand Rapids. "If Grand Rapids ever had a red light district, that was it. But you go down that road now and it's about ready to explode with all kinds of economic development. There are new businesses opening and signs about space for lease. It's a pretty exciting transformation."

When the Avenue for the Arts project began, Michigan's state government was just beginning to focus on how it might offer comprehensive assistance and incentives for such projects. Even with innovative and complicated financing that draws on historic preservation tax credits, existing state brownfield redevelopment credits, New Market Tax Credits, local tax abatements, and private donations, the nonprofit housing company behind the initiative will still wind up several million dollars in debt, according to Guy.

Even so, Dwelling Place of Grand Rapids, Inc.—the organization behind the project—and its chief operating officer, Dennis Sturtevant, are still finding creative ways to make the project a long-term success. Sturtevant said that the tax credits require the property to be maintained as a limited liability corporation or limited partnership for at least seven to eight years. One option at the end of that period will be to convert the apartments into condos for sale to individuals.

In the meantime, Sturtevant said, Dwelling Place is working with Burlington Associates, a consulting group from Vermont, to create a community land trust in Kent County. Sturtevant is hopeful that the trust will help the project benefit the community over the long term by maintaining affordability, even as property values dramatically escalate in this increasingly dynamic part of the city.

In a land trust, low- or moderate-income property buyers benefit because the purchase price is subsidized by public funds and philanthropic sources. Although a property may appraise at a high price, the land cost is subsidized, thereby lowering the purchasers' acquisition cost. The trust retains ownership of the land, but the buyer owns any improvements, and the terms of the deal limit how much appreciation an owner may take from a property when it is sold.

As a result, Sturtevant said, The Dwelling Place is assured that the resale price of any of its properties won't exceed the rise in area median income—keeping it affordable for low and moderate income households.

Andy Guy is effusive in his praise for Sturtevant, both for his ability to devise complex financing solutions and for his determination.

"He's just done some unbelievable stuff in really mining all the opportunities in state law and finding other funding. He's looked at all kinds of potential money and wired it up to where it works," Guy says.

It is a testament to the determination and vision of a number of people that downtown revitalization continues in virtually every area—despite many barriers. Governor Jennifer M. Granholm's Cool Cities initiative is designed to get the legislature to pump considerably more resources and assistance into such projects throughout Michigan.

In addition to the artist-oriented housing project, the city previously energized another section of downtown with a high-tech life sciences program. Meanwhile, the Avenue for the Arts initiative is only part of a larger revitalization of the Heartside neighborhood, which was already becoming an area known for its arts and entertainment offerings, enjoying new investment and businesses.

Remain True to the City's Uniqueness

"The companies that survive longest are the ones that work out what they uniquely can give to the world—not just growth or money, but their excellence, their respect for others, or their ability to make people happy. Some call those things a soul."

Charles Handy, from "The Search for Meaning,"
Leader to Leader (Summer 1997 issue)

What's true for companies is equally true for cities. While cities must adapt to change and the growth of global influence, a strong sense of community needs to be retained by honoring the history of the city's art, architecture, and traditions.

You can get in tune with the changing world, but you should still be able to make your own music. Cities should build on what they are and what they have—particularly those qualities that strengthen a sense of community and connections among people.

The Principle in Action

The Main Street That Killed the Mall: Winter Park, Florida

In the mid-1960s a modern marvel came to Winter Park, Florida: an enclosed, air-conditioned shopping mall. For residents of this sleepy city, it seemed like progress had really arrived. Despite the fact that the city already had a quaint and popular outdoor shopping street, Park Avenue, residents and tourists began flocking to the new mall. The Winter Park Mall thrived.

But during the late 1980s and early 1990s, the mall began losing sales and then tenants. Was a regional recession to blame? Or was it competition from other malls in the area? The real answer was found on Park Avenue. Despite a recession and increased commercial development in the region, Park Avenue continued to grow. In the words of architect Victor Dover, Park Avenue became "the Main Street that killed the mall."

How? The answer is simple: The city never gave up on its main street. Thanks to the vision of city leaders (and planner Don Martin in particular), the street was never allowed to languish. Leaders improved infrastructure, built parks and parking lots, widened sidewalks, planted trees, and were generally creative in fostering a climate that supported local businesses. Small restaurants were allowed to serve alcohol and have tables on the sidewalk. Shops were able to market their merchandise outside as well. And the city ensured that a large art festival continued to be held downtown.

Today, Park Avenue is one of the liveliest pedestrian streets in the South. While vehicular traffic on the street is encouraged, it is tamed using various measures. The brick street, which was narrowed to allow wider sidewalks, creates a rumble-strip effect, cars are allowed to park on almost every inch of curb, and pedestrian crossings are numerous.

The Town That Time Forgot, But People Didn't: Madison, Indiana

Gently perched atop a small ridge above the banks of the Ohio River, Madison, Indiana, offers a fantastic understanding of what towns used to be like. Madison also challenges us with glimpses of the kinds of towns we should be leaving behind for the benefit of future generations.

Madison was founded in 1809 as a port and supply town for settlers moving west, and the town prospered for many years. The Steamboat Era saw the town growing into its present form, but Madison was left behind when railroads became dominant.

The industrialized growth that occurred in so many railroad towns did not occur there, and the town slid instead into a century-long slumber. Because of this, most of Madison remains as it was 150 years ago—which proved to be the silver lining in the cloud that had been hanging over Madison. Its preserved architecture and town design have become its claims to fame.

Madison has the largest historic district in Indiana, containing more than a thousand 19th century structures. All 133 blocks of the downtown area fall inside the National Register district. Perhaps nowhere else in the United States is so large a 19th century town so fully intact.

Yet Madison is not just a museum of interest only to architects and historians. It is a thriving town, offering a variety of festivals, restaurants, and water-based activities, including a nationally known hydroplane race. Many one-of-a-kind bed and breakfast inns entice folks to stay and tour the town's tree-lined streets. In recent years winemaking has blossomed, and many shops invite tourists in for samples. In Madison, uniqueness has become not just an architectural signature, but also a way of life.

Some Good, Common Horse Sense: Lexington, Kentucky

The Purchase of Development Rights program in Lexington, Kentucky, is a vivid example of a city striving to remain true to what has made it great. Preserving agricultural land makes economic sense, especially in the Bluegrass with its wonderful, but limited, gift of prime soils. These soils make Lexington–Fayette County not only the agricultural king of Kentucky but also—when you count the "crop" of thoroughbred horses—of the world.

The PDR program ensures that the community will continue to attract tourists from around the globe as well as maintain a clean and green environment. The community's investment in the program demonstrates a concern for its unique heritage and maintaining its identity as the "Thoroughbred Capital of the World."

The investment also proves that Lexington is serious about downtown redevelopment. By committing funds to preserve productive agricultural land that might otherwise have been developed, the broad coalition of community leaders who crafted the PDR program presented the city with a challenge: grow downtown.

Lexington is doing just that. Business people, developers, investors, community leaders, and regular citizens have realized that the city's economic future resides not in the green fields surrounding Lexington but in its very heart. This is the message that PDR has sent. And it's a great example of how a city can do vital things to remain true to itself without sacrificing economic growth.

Lexington is also noteworthy for the Embrace Healthy Living principle because, despite being the center of one of the world's largest burley tobacco markets and having a long tradition of tolerance for, if not outright support of, smoking, it has enacted a comprehensive public smoking ban—a true sea change in attitude.

Don't Merely Grow ... Plan and Develop Over Time

"Without leaps of imagination, or dreaming, we lose the excitement of possibilities. Dreaming, after all, is a form of planning."

Gloria Steinem

I remember seeing a bumper sticker once, put out by developers, which said "GROWTH IS GOOD." Every time I saw one, I had the urge to slap on a sticker beside it that said "NOT NECESSARILY!"

Growth in and of itself has no redeeming value. Cancer, after all, is a growth. So are weeds. To simply say "growth is good" is actually to say very little.

Growth without proper planning is something to avoid. And growth without dreaming can never tap into the full range of potential. A community should discourage the kind of hasty growth that often leads to sprawl and overextends a city's ability to provide services. A community can, instead, take its time and get it right.

By first dreaming and then methodically planning, cities can enhance their quality of life while also growing. But growth for growth's sake? That's a prescription for disaster.

The Principle in Action

A Grand Vision, Cultivated Over Decades: Mariemont, Ohio

Mariemont, Ohio, is one of the most beautiful cities in the world. Like most gorgeous cities, it didn't happen by accident. It was the result of a grand vision, achieved through many years of careful planning.

Mariemont was the dream of Mary Emery, who wanted to create a model city to house industrial workers. At the turn of the 20th century, most working class housing was squalid and unhealthy. Emery envisioned a complete community of shops, offices, churches, schools, and houses in a garden setting. Her idea was inspired by the world's first garden city of Letchworth, England.

Emery hired a first-rate town planner who would guide the process from the start. The planner, John Nolen, believed that towns needed more than ordinances—more than mere words—to become beautiful. Towns also needed creative design, illustrated with pictures. To that end, his designs of streets with green medians, parks, greenways, and the town green—as well as architectural styles—were all deliberately detailed. Nothing was left to chance.

Construction began in the early 1920s. Because the plan was so detailed, there was no concern for the city's future growth. Every citizen and developer knew the desired direction, and all worked together. Thus, despite the fact that the city was not completed for more than 20 years, it retained a remarkably cohesive and beautiful character.

Sometimes It Takes Several Villages: San Diego, California

Blessed with a near perfect climate, an oceanfront location, and mountains and deserts within easy reach, San Diego, California, seems an ideal place to build the perfect city. For years, however, the city was without a vision. As a result, San Diego assumed the default future of suburban sprawl, which rapidly eroded the city's quality of life. Traffic was increasing, air quality was decreasing, and beautiful views were replaced by the standard version of Anywhere, U.S.A.

Eventually, city and community leaders had enough. Instead of continuing to rely on the growth patterns of sprawl, the city embarked on an ambitious plan to create a "City of Villages." The goal is to have San Diego evolve in harmony with its great natural setting. The village strategy was chosen because villages allow people to connect to what is important to them—jobs, education, civic uses, shopping and green spaces—in ways other than through their automobiles.

This deceptively simple strategy was developed in conjunction with the creation of a set of core city values. Thousands of citizens helped city leaders develop these statements, which included protection of the environment, creation of walkable neighborhoods with a diverse and affordable housing base, and fostering a vibrant and diverse population.

Neighborly attitudes help explain why San Diego stipulated that a 2.7-acre city park (including playground) be located just beyond the center field fence of PETCO Park, the San Diego Padres' new downtown stadium for major league baseball. Known as "the Park at the Park," the elevated grassy area offers good views of the baseball playing field and a large video screen for great coverage of the game. People pay $5 to get into the park when the Padres are playing, but it becomes a regular free city park any other time.

As a result of such community-building efforts, San Diego in 2004 was named one of America's most livable cities. Economic development continues to thrive as well. Most important, perhaps, the citizens of the city know that they finally have a lasting vision of the future.

A Radical Idea Becomes a Lesson in Brilliance: Portland, Oregon

In 1972, long before sprawl was a national concern, Portland, Oregon, took the bold step of imagining what kind of city it wanted to be in the 21st century—bold because conventional wisdom at the time insisted that a city could only plan effectively for much shorter periods, generally five to ten years.

Portland's city leaders were unfazed by such limited thinking. They dared to follow their then-city planner's advice of "We do what we can today, but it's what benefits the next century that matters."

Such radical vision has created one of the most functional, beautiful, efficient, and economically and socially diverse cities in the world. Long before gridlock occurred, Portland planned for a light rail system to move people around the city. Defying the national trend of building huge super-block type structures such as convention centers and sports arenas in downtowns, the city kept its small walkable grid of streets intact and worked hard to preserve the buildings that line them.

To counteract skyrocketing housing prices, Portland passed laws that encouraged redevelopment and infill housing. To protect rural and natural areas, the city created an urban growth boundary to prevent further sprawl.

Not resting on its laurels, Portland has plans for downtown parks and greenways—and the concept of car sharing as a way to reduce traffic, parking lot needs, and individual cost is gaining ground. In addition, more than ever before, city leaders are ensuring that citizens are completely involved in the planning process. Because of its past and its ongoing attention to the future, Portland is one of the most studied cities in the world. What once seemed radical is now regarded as brilliant planning.

Build Beautifully and Steward the Environment

"I look forward to an America which will not be afraid of grace and beauty, which will protect the beauty of our natural environment, which will preserve the great old American houses and squares and parks of our national past and which will build handsome and balanced cities for our future."

John F. Kennedy, speech at Amherst College, October 1963

Buildings and architecture reflect a community's values. By preserving buildings of historic significance and constructing new ones that are both aesthetically pleasing and functional, we strengthen a city's ability to provide a high quality of life.

President Kennedy used interesting phrasing—not to be "afraid" of grace and beauty. Sometimes it seems as if we really are averse to those things, as if in our rush to grow and compete we think success can occur only with the exclusion of aesthetics.

The irony is that, as we move farther and farther away from an industrial society to one based on information, service, and technology, the cities that make themselves aesthetically pleasing and environmentally sound are going to attract the more highly skilled and talented workers.

As place becomes less and less important in terms of being able to have an economic impact on a widespread scale, place conversely becomes more and more important in terms of people choosing where they want to live on the basis of comfort and quality of life. Those cities that make themselves attractive are more likely to lure entrepreneurs and skilled workers who can boost the local economy.

The Principle in Action

Cleaning Up Your Act With Architectural Aesthetics: Bath, England

The city of Bath, England, represents the power of an idea to shape a city. In Bath, as in a few other places (Paris and Washington, D.C., for instance), a great thought has been given physical form. In the case of Bath, the idea was that a city should reflect classical order and beauty. This idea was expressed primarily through Georgian architecture. The result is a city of great and lasting beauty.

Bath is an old town. Long before the Romans came in 43 AD, ancient people had been gathering to bathe in its hot springs. Bath had an early era of prosperity in the late Middle Ages, but experienced a long decline as English society discounted the value of the hot spring waters.

It was Queen Anne who rediscovered the value of the waters in the late 17th century. Since a visit to Bath was again fashionable for the cream of English society, some enterprising men undertook to promote their construction talents by redeveloping the town.

Foremost among them were the Woods, John the Elder and John the Younger. The elder planned and the younger built. To them we owe gratitude for the creation of the Royal

Crescent and the Circus. The impact of these two groups of buildings in the Palladian style (later renamed Georgian) was profound.

Other developers began projects in hopes of imitating the Woods' success. These in turn inspired more building in the same style. Soon the entire town had been transformed. This transformation led to a revival. Poets and writers such as Wordsworth, Dickens, and Jane Austen were attracted to Bath's beauty and order. Painters and architects traveled far to capture the essence of the town. Great leaders sought inspiration along its streets and parks. This renaissance is still occurring today—and all because a great idea was expressed in the making of a town.

Of Hydrogen Aplomb and the Bus Electric: Europe and Santa Monica, California

As concerns about the use of expensive, polluting, non-renewable fossil fuels rise, cities around the world are seeking alternatives. For example, several European cities are testing fleets of hydrogen buses. These buses use fuel cells that generate energy from hydrogen for an electric motor. This fuel also makes the buses cleaner and quieter.

The electricity needed to produce hydrogen can be provided in different ways; hydroelectric, wind, geothermal, and solar power are some of the sources being used. Eventually these European cities hope to decrease, if not eliminate, their dependence on imported oil.

In California, the government of Santa Monica has instituted what it calls the Sustainable City Program. Santa Monica defines a sustainable city as one that can meet its current needs without compromising the ability of future generations to do the same.

Under this program, the city requires that 75 percent of its fleet operate on alternative fuels. These include electricity, compressed natural gas (CNG), and liquefied natural gas (LNG). Each has a distinct use. Electric vehicles are used for short distances with flat terrain, such as downtown shuttles. CNG is used for heavy-duty, medium distance needs such as garbage trucks, and LNG is used for longer-range vehicles such as city buses.

The city's alternative fuel infrastructure currently consists of eight electric charging stations and one large CNG facility. Plans are underway for an LNG facility. When complete, Santa Monica's initiative may prove that electricity and natural gas are viable alternatives to petroleum-based fuels.

Long on Green:
Seattle, Washington

After more than 5,000 years of existence, humans have finally learned that cities can sometimes be hard on the environment. Air and water pollution are two of the chief problems. Throughout much of history, cities generally just passed along the problems downwind or downstream. But in the 21st century, New Cities will be those that steward the environment.

A new way of thinking about cities and their relationship to the environment is gaining ground: green infrastructure. The term refers to an interconnected network of green spaces planned and managed for the reduction of air and water pollution. This network also extends to green buildings, which use design elements and materials to lessen their impact on renewable and non-renewable resources. Together, green buildings and green infrastructure increase a city's quality of life.

Several cities have adopted progressive green measures to improve the environment as well as to reduce costs. For instance, Seattle is seeking to become as renowned for green infrastructure and building as it is for coffee, software development, and its music scene. Seattle is currently focusing on alternative storm water management systems. In a national first-of-its-kind project, the city—collaborating with residents and the state department of transportation—created landscaped edges along certain streets to filter and slow storm water runoff into adjacent creeks.

As the world becomes ever more urbanized, environmental sensitivity will become ever more important to city life and economic success. Seattle is already taking big steps to stay on top of this important area.

They Built This City on (Neighborhood) Block 'n Soul: The Village of West Clay, Indiana

Just north of Indianapolis, amid tedious more-of-the-same suburban development, a new neighborhood is taking shape. Barely two years old, The Village of West Clay stands as a beacon to people seeking not just a home but a community with a soul.

The experienced builders of the village are farsighted but not completely altruistic. They realize that buyers are increasingly searching for long-term value, both economic and personal. Understanding this, the developers have moved to build true neighborhoods, and West Clay proves that they know more is involved than building fancy entry gates or devising pretentious subdivision names.

The core values at West Clay are traditional ones—most evident in the domestic and commercial architecture that is modeled on historic Indiana towns. The buildings in the Village Center look as if they belong in a 150-year-old town.

Beyond the architecture lies a philosophy that development should put people first. This value is demonstrated in many ways. For example, there is a mix of land uses that will allow parents to send their children around the corner on a quick errand or elderly residents to make a short car trip to the store.

These values extend to the variety of housing sizes and prices. Apartments over stores exist down the block from large single-family homes and across the street from a row of townhouses. This mix creates all kinds of opportunities. Perhaps grandparents and grandchildren will be able to live within the same neighborhood. Maybe a young teacher can get his start in a loft above a set of offices.

Another example of this "people first" attitude is the front porch. Houses are built with front porches close to the street so neighbors can get to know each other. Front porch sitters also act as a private security force, watching the street and keeping it safe. This is a far cry from the garage-door-dominated streetscapes of conventional suburbia.

Protection of the environment is another value. More than 160 acres within the development are protected as open space for the enjoyment of the residents. Throughout the village are small parks within easy walking distance for children. With walking encouraged, the health of residents is improved, and the air is perhaps a bit cleaner. For shade on hot days, trees line each thoroughfare.

Although civic and social spaces are the focus of the village, the values of the community are balanced with the provision of privacy for residents. Backyards are enclosed and private. Individual homes provide a quiet refuge amid many amenities. But when someone wants a break from solitude, a social club with a swimming pool beckons. And the village square and green are perfect backdrops for weddings and community parties.

The Village of West Clay is no quaint replica of a time long gone. The developers view it as a way to outsell the competition, which they are doing. The quality of life premium per square foot is increasing rapidly. Although these rising costs could thwart the efforts to mix age and income groups, a similar development nearby might have the ability to stem the increase.

All in all, however, local government considers it smart growth. Consumers see real estate appreciation beyond what they can get in look-alike subdivisions. And most important, the people who live there have found a great place to call home.

Recruit, Retain, and Generate Wealth

"The gratification of wealth is not found in mere possession or in lavish expenditure, but in its wise application."

Miguel de Cervantes, from *Don Quixote de la Mancha*

By offering reasonable incentives to nurture existing businesses and attract new ones, cities can generate wealth that can be directed to quality of life enhancements.

Money often gets a bad rap. We call it filthy lucre or complain about crass materialism. And while greed can lead to serious problems, as the scandal at Enron demonstrated, deep down we all know how important financial success and stability are to each of us individually and to our communities collectively. After all, money only represents other assets we have. It represents the minerals we have extracted from the ground or the crops we have grown or the machines and services and inventions we have devised.

Wealth, both fiscal and social, is a laudable goal. Wealth can eliminate need, ease suffering, and enhance opportunities. Cities can do a lot both directly and indirectly to increase wealth. They can offer reasonable incentives to nurture existing businesses and attract new ones. They can work closely with the business community to build reliable infrastructure and improve efficiency. They can adjust the regulatory environment to encourage industry and commerce. Most important, they can recognize and appreciate the critical role the private sector plays in building New Cities.

No city (or person) need be slave to the almighty dollar, but only the most narrow-minded citizen will fail to see that wealth in a community means greater opportunities for all kinds of amenities, from symphony orchestras to inspiring architecture to holiday decorations to needed services. New Cities nurture assets that provide jobs, jobs provide wealth, and wealth can, and should, be used to benefit the community.

Wealth is basically only problematic when it is used by special interests that have an abundance of it to advance their own narrow concerns without regard for the health and vitality of the community. But when commerce, citizens, and city hall cooperate to enhance the wealth of a community for the benefit of all, wealth can be the driving force behind progressive change.

The Principle in Action

Onward and UPSward: Louisville, Kentucky

When United Parcel Service officials named the company's new package processing facility UPS Worldport, they weren't kidding. Dubbed "the Versailles of Global Commerce," the 4 million square foot facility in Louisville, Kentucky, processes an average of 600,000 packages per day—then sends them on their merry global way via a fleet of jets (approximately 100 takeoffs and landings daily). One presumes a brown truck or two is also involved.

The numbers are staggering. The facility cost $1 billion to build and houses 17,000 conveyor systems that, stretched out, would cover 122 miles. UPS Worldport is capable of sorting 304,000 packages every hour and on peak days has processed in excess of 1.3 million packages.

When UPS came to Louisville 20 years earlier, its original facility sorted about 2,000 packages daily. What eventually has become Worldport has also become a world-class partnership among the company, the city, and the University of Louisville.

UPS embraced the concept of working with local community and academic leaders, creating a training institute at the university, hiring and training local people to qualify for new jobs that were still being created, and working with local government to create a unified economic vision. In all, UPS' 23,000 jobs have a half-billion-dollar impact on the local economy.

Retaining a company like UPS and providing incentives for dramatic expansion is just one example of how Louisville's leaders are implementing the economic philosophy of taking care of their own.

The regional community also bought into the concept of connecting to a future global village that in many respects is already becoming reality. Greater Louisville, Inc., comprised of a cross-section of leaders in the region surrounding Louisville, has actively pursued a strategy of business recruitment and retention that places start-up companies in areas that make sense without regard to local politics. As a result, the entire region is reaping the benefits.

When Louisville recently merged city and county governments, the city suddenly became the nation's 16th largest. That statistical growth is being matched by visionary growth.

The People-Friendly Juggernaut:
Sioux Falls, South Dakota

Sioux Falls may not be the city that immediately comes to mind when you think of economic juggernauts, but perhaps it should be. This medium-sized city in America's heartland has received accolades from the likes of *Forbes* and *Inc.* magazines for its ability to recruit, retain, and generate wealth.

The secret, suggests Dan Hindbjorgen, is simple.

"We're all about putting people first," says Hindbjorgen, vice president of the Sioux Falls Development Foundation. "The cornerstone of our economic success hinges on people and positive relationships."

There are other elements at work. South Dakota's business-friendly tax structure and Sioux Falls' knack for sensing future business trends have worked to the city's advantage for the past 20 years. The results have been phenomenal. Major corporations have relocated here. Local business is expanding and booming. And in early 2004, unemployment stood at only 2.9 percent. You have to wonder, is it something in the water?

Actually, the success flows from the collective knowledge of some savvy citizens. These visionaries have built a very simple but effective model to grow businesses. They start with a tax climate that encourages growth and expansion;

partner with educational and vocational institutions to tailor curriculum to business community needs; create a land base that makes business development and expansion affordable; and provide the same incentives to local companies that they do to relocating companies.

The result is a rapidly expanding homegrown economy. Sioux Falls Forward, a group of people committed to the community's economic well being, regularly visits with company leaders and employees to assess their needs and concerns and encourages their participation in the process.

"We take care of our people and give them every reason to stay here," Hindbjorgen says. "Economic development is not just about recruiting new companies. It's mostly about caring for the ones that you already have."

That's a lesson all cities should learn.

There's NOBIDness Like This Business: New Orleans, Louisiana

Created in 1979, NOBID—the New Orleans Business and Industrial District—was carved out of 7,000 acres of prime real estate near downtown. Armed with incentives, a business incubator program, port access, and a client list of more than 110 of America's most prestigious companies,

NOBID was one of the first initiatives that raised the bar for wealth generation among the world's major urban centers.

To recruit and retain business, New Orleans offers a virtually complete business toolkit. Eligible start-up companies can receive financing and business development expertise while rubbing shoulders with the likes of NASA, Folgers Coffee, and CSX. New Orleans sells the concept of "moving and shaking" and backs it up with incentive packages to improve the prospects of success for entrepreneurs and corporate giants alike. NOBID also draws on more than 50 vocational education facilities in the area to provide a qualified workforce.

Overcome Obstacles

"The majority see the obstacles; the few see the objectives; history records the successes of the latter, while oblivion is the reward of the former."

Alfred A. Montapert

Once obstacles can be recognized as opportunities, they become catalysts for positive change. By turning problems into engines for change, creative thinking takes over. It's important that cities seek solutions from unexpected sources—and also look to other communities to see if they have overcome a similar problem, and how they did it.

The Principle in Action

Pardon Me, Boy, Is That the Chattanooga Cleanup? Chattanooga, Tennessee

It was as if the Chattanooga Choo Choo had come to a screeching halt smack in the middle of town, belching black smoke that billowed, spread, and settled into the valleys surrounding the city. It was always there, turning daytime sky into sickly blackness and nighttime dreams into visions of pollutants dancing in people's heads.

That was the grim reality of Chattanooga, which by 1969 had earned the dubious distinction of being named the dirtiest city in America by the Environmental Protection Agency. "We had a heart-attack situation," City Council Chairman David Crockett told *U.S. News*.

It really was that bad. People would drive with their lights on in the dimness that passed for daylight. And the bad times persisted, extending all the way into the early 1980s. By then downtown had pretty much flat lined.

Finally, people had had enough. Things were so rundown (in addition to virtually no population growth and ongoing job layoffs), it seemed restoring the city might be too formidable a challenge. But leaders and volunteers were in it for the long haul, smart enough and dedicated enough to know that they would have to be.

That was clear in the name they chose for the task force formed to find solutions. Vision 2000 recognized that it might take almost two decades to reverse all the dirty trends. Vision 2000 was privately funded and inclusive—calling on citizens, economic development groups, and public/private partnerships to envision what Chattanooga should become by the 21st century.

First was getting rid of the pollution, which the city has managed in such impressive fashion that the United Nations University and the Zero Emissions Research Initiative held its Second World Congress on Zero Emissions in Chattanooga in 1996. That year, local officials went to Istanbul, Turkey, to receive a best practices award from the UN for the city's environmental accomplishments.

Chattanooga continues to improve. The city now has the largest electric bus fleet in the nation. A privately funded $45 million aquarium that opened in 1992 has boosted tourism. Art districts, riverfront development along a fifteen-mile stretch of the Tennessee River, housing renovations, and green space development are just part of the ongoing effort.

Giving Chattanooga a complete makeover was the result of the work of a large number of determined and dedicated people. One key contributor was Jack Lupton, whose personal donations and money from the family's Lyndhurst Foundation was the catalyst behind the funding for downtown renovation.

Turning Post-Oil Boom Blahs Into Diversified Success: Tulsa, Oklahoma

For decades Tulsa, Oklahoma, enjoyed the prosperity of a town whose economic muscle focused on the considerable flex of oil and natural gas giants such as Phillips and Williams. But after the oil speculation boom of the early 1980s created a record number of jobs, the prosperity began to wither.

That's when the Williams Companies (now known as Williams) sought innovative answers. In 1986 Williams turned its existing natural gas and oil pipelines into conduits for fiber optic lines—its electronic communications network eventually connecting more than 125 cities and covering about 32,000 miles. In addition, the company now owns more than two million square feet of data housing space.

Williams still is involved in oil and gas, but its leap into the Information Age by taking its old infrastructure and adapting it for high-speed data transmission set a tone for the entire city of Tulsa.

Although big oil and natural gas remain a key part of the city's economy, Tulsa is far more diversified—with a number of public-private partnerships that have spurred economic development in such areas as aeronautics, telecommunications, manufacturing, and service. The Tulsa Metro Chamber says that the number of jobs in the city has far surpassed even the heady days of Big Oil.

From Rocky Situation to Total Renovation: Sandy Hook, Kentucky

Nobody had much reason to visit Sandy Hook anymore. A small town located on the Big Sandy River in Eastern Kentucky, Sandy Hook had little to offer its residents, much less its visitors.

But the phoenix, it turns out, isn't the only thing that can rise from its ashes. The Sandy Hook of today boasts a new post office; a renovated courthouse; a sleek and modern building housing a library, technology center, and human resources center; and a new school complex that includes an elementary school, middle school, and high school—complete with indoor swimming pool and fitness center.

The city also renovated buildings to attract new business, worked to secure highway construction to improve its accessibility, and created partnerships with the University of Kentucky and Morehead State University to provide vocational services.

There's also the Laurel Gorge Culture and Heritage Center on Laurel Creek just outside the city, which is attracting tourists and becoming a source of community and regional pride. More than $190 million has been invested in Sandy Hook, and it has created 350 new jobs while also helping to engage its citizenry.

How did a small isolated place in Eastern Kentucky become so skilled at New City ideas? The short answer is citizenship—with people such as Representative Rocky Adkins, Elliott County School Superintendent Eugene Binion, Mayor Robby Adkins, County Judge-Executive Charles Pennington, the local bank, and several other business and property owners.

"My old college coach used to tell me 'Don't ever be satisfied,'" Representative Adkins says. "And I'm not. We're striving every day to be better."

Most of those behind Sandy Hook's rebirth grew up in the community or its environs. After decades of decline and watching young people leave, they decided to act.

The catalyst came when U.S. postal officials decided to build a new post office, but not downtown. Most folks wanted it to remain there, perhaps aware that if the post office left, the city had little going for it. With assistance from the Kentucky League of Cities and several others, Sandy Hook fought the move and eventually won. Beyond the result itself, the dedicated effort by so many heralded the rebirth of the city as a community.

Somehow it is fitting that the state legislator who helped get this community turned around is named Rocky. Much like the Rocky Balboa of filmdom, this was a town that didn't even appear to have a puncher's chance at winning. But it fought back, in a big way.

Rethink Boundaries

"Millions of men have lived to fight, build palaces and boundaries, shape destinies and societies; but the compelling force of all times has been the force of originality and creation profoundly affecting the roots of human spirit."

Ansel Adams

Business gurus have called it "the death of distance." The electronic era has linked us in ways that provide instant communication and global connection. And with this new terrain comes the possibility for cities to drop boundaries and join with other communities when it benefits them.

These boundaries can be symbolic as well as literal. A few decades ago, academia was pretty much divorced from commerce. But now we find several examples of business, education, and government collaborating to improve the quality of life of communities.

Whether it's seeking partnerships with businesses, surrounding communities, or other local governments, thinking beyond one's boundaries can help a city thrive.

The Principle in Action

Dogs Run Free:
The Communities of King County, Washington

When dog owners in the outlying area of Seattle, Washington, wanted to find a place where dogs could run free, a number of communities, organizations, and individuals in King County dropped boundaries to create a common off-leash park area for all in the region to use.

The cities of SeaTac, Federal Way, Auburn, Des Moines, Kent, Burien, Renton, and Tukwila refurbished Grandview Park, a 37-acre facility located in SeaTac with views of Mount Rainier and the Green River valley. Because it also is convenient to major highways, people in the surrounding towns can easily and quickly access the park.

In addition to cooperation among the cities and King County government—all of which provided funds, labor, and equipment—a number of organizations and individuals also partnered to make the off-leash park a reality, including volunteer groups from the Boeing company, local banks and churches, and boy scout troops. Volunteers from an organization called Serve Our Dog Area (SODA) maintain the park itself.

When the park opened, the *Seattle Post-Intelligencer* said its creation "seemed to be a textbook case of cooperation." It is the very sort of reaching beyond local boundaries for the common good that New Cities are adept at practicing.

Easing the Blues in the Bluegrass: Central Kentucky

The formation of Bluegrass Tomorrow in 1988 was a then-unique regional approach in Kentucky that has since caused other regions, both in the state and across the country, to broaden their thinking to grow their economies and improve their quality of life. The key: cooperative efforts among communities.

Bluegrass Tomorrow's founders recognized that people needed to see how community decisions reached beyond their local boundaries to affect an entire region—and that by working together they could plan and execute more positive outcomes.

Bluegrass Tomorrow brought together more than a dozen community leaders, covering agricultural, business, preservation, and growth concerns from seven counties in a metropolitan area of more than 500,000 people. They joined in voicing concern for the future of one of the world's great cultural landscape regions: the Bluegrass area of Central Kentucky.

These private-sector leaders knew that the most cherished values of the region—beautiful green spaces, distinct towns, scenic roads, and environmental and fiscal resources—were threatened by default decisions made by local governments and a largely unregulated private market.

They envisioned a different future—one that would welcome change, but avoid the senseless sacrifice of those aesthetic values. They believed that change was possible simply because of who they were and the power of the vision they would create.

By creating the first nonprofit regional planning group in Kentucky, these leaders expanded the understanding of the region. In linking the region to geographic and not political boundaries, local leaders and citizens were better able to gauge the larger impact of local decisions.

The coalescence of these individuals is a prime example of rethinking another type of boundary as well. Despite having greatly disparate backgrounds, these leaders understood early that each of their individual interests stood to suffer from current practices and trends in the region.

For example, large banks, although often thought of as purely pro-growth with no regard for aesthetic or environmental values, partnered with thoroughbred horse farm owners to decry the loss of prime farmlands. Environmentalists, meanwhile, understood that by implementing new tools to direct new development, the region's fragile ecosystems could be better protected. Homebuilders, commercial developers, and their boosters recognized that protecting the region's quality of life would ensure continued success of their industries. And the region's largest employer, Toyota Motor Manufacturing, Kentucky, Inc., knew that smarter planning was critical to the long-term success of its nearly $2 billion investment in the region.

The result has been smarter growth as local towns think beyond their boundaries and understand the systemic relationship they have with others in the area.

Buy Locally, Sell Globally

"A true community maximizes the potential of whatever human resources exist within it...by allowing for all possible combinations."

Philip Slater, from *Earthwalk*

Supporting local businesses helps pump up the local economy. And creating a local business that sells to a global audience can increase the force of that pumping considerably.

In addition to contributing to the local economy, this principle concerns itself with loyalty to the community, charitable giving, and political involvement.

The Principle in Action

Fruit of the Vine...at Your Door: Portsmouth, Rhode Island

John Barstow of Boston happened upon an area in Portsmouth, Rhode Island, in the early 1860s that would become Greenvale Farm. Barstow built this rural retreat near the city of Portsmouth with some guidance from landscape theorist Richard Morris Copeland's book, *Country Life*. He wanted to establish a "rural agricultural retreat, but one that would provide occupation as well as recreation," as set out in Copeland's work.

Greenvale Farm was renowned for its prize-winning livestock throughout the 20th century, but it would make a remarkable transformation. Barstow probably could never have envisioned Greenvale becoming a premier New England winery, but that's what his great-great-great-niece and nephew began to make it in 1993. They started first as growers for a large winery but eventually established their own.

Today, with a production capacity of 5,000 cases annually, Greenvale Farm is ready to reach far beyond the boundaries of Portsmouth. The winery has gone global, via the Internet. Wine enthusiasts anywhere in the world can enjoy the crisp Chardonnay or Cabernet Franc simply by clicking to the farm's online retail store.

Selling locally produced wine via the Internet to bring in global dollars that are spent locally is a classic NewCities way for communities to sell in the worldwide environment while stimulating the local economy.

Of course, Greenvale Farms isn't the only business reaching an international wine market. The wine industry as a whole has taken the global Internet community by storm. It is now possible to experience the wines of the world through a few clicks of the mouse (a valid credit card helps, of course). But what matters is that big moneymakers can thrive in small places via global connections and sales—and in so doing help that small place to survive. Greenvale was no longer productive as a farm, but is thriving as a winery with a worldwide clientele.

We live in a world of big box retail and far-flung global corporate operations that often threaten to suck local economies dry. But entrepreneurs always respond to the challenge through inventive and creative ways. Sometimes the answer resides in a virtual state, right at the doorstep of the city/county line. Just ask the folks in Portsmouth and the owners of Greenvale.

Selling Outside of the Box:
San Diego, California

San Diego has been mentioned previously as an example of employing a NewCities principle ("Don't Merely Grow… Plan and Develop Over Time"), but, as is the case with most progressive cities, several principles usually come into play. San Diego is a good example, given that it has also made huge strides in its economy by connecting to the outside world. Evertek Computer Corporation is one of the city's companies that has led the way.

Evertek is not your typical locally-owned business. The computer component reseller has been setting trends since 1990. It was one of the first companies to use fax broadcasting (followed by email broadcasting) and the very first to have a video email broadcast, in 1997.

As early as 1990, San Diego and its business community began searching for ways to retain homegrown entrepreneurs while opening global markets as a means to expand its economic base.

With encouragement from the city and the San Diego Chamber of Commerce, local businesses were among the first in the world to go global via the Internet. As a result, businesses as diverse as biotech, hypersonic sound engineering, and environmental systems management are succeeding.

Evertek scored a major coup when it joined the U.S. Government Export Portal's buyusa.com e-commerce group in 2001. Boasting 107 national companies and 157 foreign companies, buyusa.com has been the catalyst for Evertek's burgeoning global trade. More than ten foreign companies from as many countries have been added to the roster of corporate clients since Evertek joined buyusa.com. Foreign exports now account for more than 20 percent of Evertek's business, and that number is growing.

With business-savvy entrepreneurs and visionary city and community leaders, San Diego is boosting its local economy by thinking globally. They're not only thinking outside the box, they're selling outside the box, too.

CHAPTER THREE

WHAT A COMMUNITY PATRIOT NEEDS TO DO

By now I hope you have seen the merit in becoming a Community Patriot and are in tune with the Twelve Principles of Ongoing Success that can help you and others create a New City. But how exactly can you go about *doing* it?

First, encourage others to join you—and expect their initial response to be one of exasperation. The task seems overwhelming for many people, but good things can happen through patience and persistence.

It is best to begin with the fundamentals, and we perform the most fundamental act of democracy by electing people and holding them accountable, or by running for office ourselves. But the lack of civic engagement by ordinary people—as evidenced by a decline in voter turnout, among other symptoms —is a clear sign that American democracy is in trouble.

Curtis Gans, director of the Committee for the Study of the American Electorate, wrote in *The Washington Monthly Online* in 2000 that the United States ranked 139th out of 163 democracies in voter participation. His organization notes that the 1996 presidential election drew only 49 percent of eligible voters, the lowest turnout since 1924.

Statistics like that are bad enough, but the picture turns bleaker when you hear what so many ordinary people are saying: "I can't make a difference."… "No one will listen to me."… "Those dummies (in elected office) don't know what they're doing." This is usually followed by, "Why can't they fix things?"

When overall voting numbers are down, the potential for narrow special interests or single-issue groups to unduly influence elections is greater. For the democratic process to remain healthy, we must be true to the ideals of the representative democracy that have served us well for more than two centuries. And more people must get involved.

We began this book by talking about our changing world. In the early days of our democracy, people lived, worked, and died within fifteen miles of their birthplace. Over the 228-year course of our history, that picture has changed dramatically. With the advent of the automobile, the airplane, and even the suburbs following World War II, we learned to live farther and farther away from our birthplace. And now the new frontier is the Internet, which increasingly allows us to live and work almost anywhere we choose.

While place is increasingly less important in terms of being able to connect to the world economically, intellectually, and socially, a strong sense of local place remains important. We will, after all, still live and work and raise our children around those living next door to us—somewhere. Globalization is a reality, but we remain intertwined from neighborhood to neighborhood, community to community, state to state, and nation to nation. And our local place is still the prime source of our nurturance.

Actions at the local level are more important than ever, but only if they are relevant to the broader world. Conversely, the actions of other communities are more important to our local lives than ever before. The paradox of the 21st century is that as the world has grown more global, local becomes even more important—or, as Larry Rasmussen put it in *Moral Fragments and Moral Community*: "The more 'planetary' our lives become, the more necessary small communities are."

Numerous communities have spent countless hours and civic capital on projects only to find that they were not connected to the bigger picture and thus were doomed to fail. The recent spate of downtown revitalization projects across the nation provides an example. Many of these will fail if they are not done in a way that reflects the needs of an entire community or considers regional impact.

Downtowns are not what they once were. For decades they were the commercial and nerve center of every community. Today, the crowded parking lots of the big box stores on the edge of town offer evidence that most people have shunned downtown for convenient parking, lower prices, and the dependability of large chain stores.

Downtowns, then, must be redefined within the context of what people find appealing in the big box stores while filling a community need. An engaged citizenry must recognize that every town, no matter how small or large, needs a heart and soul—a center of its being. It is up to Community Patriots to determine whether that center is a traditional downtown or one that is reshaped to meet new needs.

There is no single answer for what works. Los Angeles, for instance, is essentially a series of several downtowns dispersed over a large area. Chicago, on the other hand, has its Magnificent Mile, where stores and restaurants surrounded by affluent neighborhoods anchor downtown and reportedly attract 25 million tourists annually. Both cities are thriving, centered communities, but in vastly different ways.

To begin reshaping a city or town, the Community Patriot begins his or her work by taking a figurative aerial snapshot of the community. This snapshot should be taken both at close range and from a much higher altitude, where the views show how the community fits into its milieu. From that perspective, an important question is: What are the community's regional attributes, and how does it fit into its state and the nation and world? (For example, homeland security risks for New York City are vastly different from those of heartland cities).

Community Patriots can band together to review the Twelve Principles and (1) assess strengths and weaknesses of the community and (2) develop a plan of action. Then it becomes a matter of putting that action plan in motion. A Community Patriot realizes that the journey to be a New City never ends. A living, thriving place has much in common with a person. It evolves, it grows, it suffers setbacks. But, much as a healthy person with a healthy outlook, it regains its footing and regenerates itself. It creates a climate of leadership for today and tomorrow.

There is one final quality that is essential to being a Community Patriot, that which was perhaps best represented by Dr. Martin Luther King, Jr. He believed that he would succeed in his efforts on behalf of civil rights, regardless of the opposition he encountered. He used his charisma and his gifts as a speaker to convince others of the rightness of the cause and the likelihood of success if people remained steadfast.

It is such steadfast belief in a cause that Community Patriots must bring to their work. It is belief in community life that allows the Community Patriot to look beyond the smugness that is so often seen in status quo civic activists who think that their community is just fine despite an obvious need for new thinking and new solutions.

A Community Patriot is a new kind of thinker. A speaker at a National League of Cities conference a few short months after September 11, 2001, noted that five things were different on the morning of September 12:

1. Little things mattered.
2. Little people mattered.
3. Authenticity mattered.
4. People were saying hello in elevators and on the street.
5. Partisanship went out the window.

But those things, the speaker lamented, disappeared just as quickly. As basic and simple as those five things are, they are vitally important, and we can ill afford for them to remain lost. As Community Patriots, we are charged with regaining these qualities, for it is the simple things—having a basic respect for people and understanding that we all want fulfilling lives—that can guide us to creating better cities, towns, and communities.

I am reminded of another personal story that underscores how the smallest of symbols can demonstrate the enduring importance of community life. When my son Ross graduated from Centre College, a small and highly regarded private college in Kentucky, he was permitted to choose one person to pay tribute to in the school's annual honor walk. The walk consisted of holding the honoree by the hand and leading him or her across the lawn of the oldest and most venerable building on campus.

My son chose my father, who grew up poor and uneducated, left Kentucky to work the factories of the North, and returned to care for my boys.

I was overwhelmed as I watched the two of them make this brief but profound walk—my son so self assured, my father awkward, frail, and uncomfortable, not knowing what to do or where to go, but walking hand in hand with his grandson. I thought of all the hard work and sacrifice my parents had made for me and for my children. I thought about just how much they had contributed to their grandson's achievement.

And there they walked, the 84-year-old man with the 22-year-old man—one with an eighth-grade education, the other with a scholarship to law school. Despite all the obvious differences, the bond between them was palpable.

And so it is with community life. We come together— young and old, rich and poor, educated and uneducated—and realize that we can only succeed if we walk together.

There are hopeful signs that we *are* learning to walk again. Some surveys show that even the huge numbers of young people who are turning away from partisan politics nevertheless are interested in community service. The key is to give them hope that they can make a difference and the means to do it.

There is a growing, healthy movement that finds people expressing concern about the state of the world's affairs—not in a partisan way, but as a desire to find solutions for a world that seems increasingly dangerous and out of control. We seek safety and stability, and more and more of us want to find it in community.

Some great thinkers have observed that the answer to global strife ironically can be found in an almost counter-intuitive way, by making local places stronger. More than once I have heard people express a desire to find a third way to escape the world of politics as usual that our stagnant two-party system has produced.

Regardless of how political structures may change or movements emerge, at the heart of it all is commitment to democratic ideals. It is a responsibility that each of us must accept if our cities, towns, and communities are to thrive.

We need to revisit what "of the people, by the people, for the people" really means and demand that community good be placed ahead of private interest. We need to shun empty rhetoric and demand accountability. We need to create a climate of healthy debate where opposing views are truly heard and compromise is encouraged.

Most of all, we need people who will be leaders. To become a Community Patriot is to recommit to this grand American experiment that remains, after all, a work in progress. We need to reestablish trust in the system and in each other. It has never come easy. It will not now. While there is no quick fix, with perseverance great things can be accomplished.

To pursue happiness is to accept that the road will often be rough. Together, in community, we can make the journey a smoother one for each of us. Together, we can breathe new life into our cities and strengthen the pulse of American democracy.

APPENDIX

Additional NewCities® Foundation Resources and Website

If you wish to contact the NewCities Foundation for more information on becoming a Community Patriot and making your community a New City, call toll free, 888-352-0922, or visit the Foundation's website at www.newcities.org.

On the website, you will also find links to various NewCities related publications, workshops, and events held by our Leadership Training Center and other resources and services—including stories of cities that are currently applying NewCities principles.

Applying the NewCities® Principles:
Is Your City a New City?

What follows is a checklist that provides ways to measure a New City. Other factors might also be appropriate, but this checklist offers a good starting point to judge how far along your city is in becoming a New City.

Please read these items and ask yourself, "How is my city doing?" The issues covered here can be a launching pad for your involvement as a Community Patriot.

Keep in mind that these questions are an informal guide for citizens and city leaders. Not all measurement criteria will apply to all cities, and success will not depend on satisfying every measure.

One thing is key: Thinking about your city's future in these terms is essential if you want to build a vibrant, healthy community.

THE TWELVE PRINCIPLES CHECKLIST

1. Connect to the World – Cities and citizens must expand their horizons to include global markets and to embrace global citizens in the community.

- Does your community work with its regional neighbors on such issues as transportation, economic development, the environment, and infrastructure?
- Does your community have an active international Sister City relationship?
- Does your city aggressively encourage foreign investment?
- Is your city wired for the 21st century?
- Is an airport with good travel connections accessible to your community?
- Do your local media provide international news?
- Is your community open to cultural diversity?
- Do your residents travel to other cities, states, and countries to learn about other cultures?

2. Cultivate Leadership and Civic Involvement – Engaged citizens assume all kinds of roles. Whether they serve as elected local officials, civic leaders, or community volunteers, involved citizens strengthen a city.

- Does your community foster and encourage civic involvement?
- Are your citizens instilled with a sense of duty to the community?
- Do most people vote?
- Are public meetings held often, and are they well attended?
- Does your community have active neighborhood associations?
- Does your community have strong local leaders with bipartisan attitudes and a spirit of cooperation?
- Does your community have local heroes who have helped the city and its citizens?
- Does your local government partner with schools, colleges, and vocational training centers to offer learning opportunities about government?
- Do your local elected offices and city-appointed boards include members who are under the age of 35?
- Is there a progressive turnover among the leadership of your city council and boards who offer fresh ideas and diverse viewpoints?

- Does your city have a leadership development program?
- Does your city government televise or webcast public meetings?
- Does your city government have a website or newsletter to keep the public informed?

3. Embrace Healthy Living – Healthy communities encourage a healthy population.

- Is your community environmentally healthy?
- Are residents in your community health conscious?
- Does your community have public parks, walking tracks, bicycle paths, and/or facilities for citizens to exercise and encourage healthy lifestyles?
- Does your community offer walkable neighborhoods (i.e., homes located within walking distance of schools, parks, grocery stores, churches)?
- Do your community's eating establishments offer healthy options?
- Does your community have limitations on cigarette smoking in restaurants and public places?
- Does your community offer extensive recreational activities for youth?

4. Encourage Youth, Diversity, and Inclusiveness — When a community recognizes youth, diversity, and inclusiveness as an important part of its fabric, individuals in that community are better prepared to deal with the larger world.

- Are young adults staying in and moving to your community?
- Is your community known as a great place to retire?
- Are festivals and entertainment a large part of the community on a year-round basis?
- Does your community actively support local musicians, writers, and artists?
- Is your community tolerant of alternative lifestyles?
- Do alternative media flourish?
- Does your community teach or cater to second languages?
- Does your community have a fairness ordinance for housing and employment?

5. Feed the Mind and Nurture the Soul – Citizens must commit to lifelong learning, including exposure to the cultural amenities that nurture the soul.

- Does your community value education and educated people?
- Does your community provide adult education programs?
- Does your community have a community college, university, or vocational education facility?
- Are there community education/leadership training opportunities?
- Does your community have museums, libraries, and history centers?
- Are there storytellers?
- Are the arts a significant part of your community image?
- Does your community have an active forum or community gathering place to discuss important issues (for example, town hall meetings)?
- Does your community provide resources for spiritual renewal?
- Does your community listen to visionaries?
- Does your community encourage youth to speak out on issues—and are they heard?
- Does your community embrace religious diversity?
- Do people regard your community as home?

6. Remain True to the City's Uniqueness – Honor the history of the city's art, architecture, and traditions. Cities must build on who they are and what they have.

- Does your community have a permanent greenbelt to prevent sprawl and protect its identity?
- Does your community actively promote historic preservation?
- Does your city support local businesses, artists, and crafts people?
- Does your community encourage and support downtown redevelopment?
- Does your community have architectural design codes to ensure historically sensitive remodeling?
- Is there an active historical society in your community?
- Does your community have distinctive landmarks or unique festivals?
- Is there an active, positive dialogue about your community's identity?
- Does your city protect its natural setting?

7. Don't Merely Grow...Plan and Develop Over Time

There is a delicate balance between size and quality of life that must remain intact.

- Does your community require small parks in new developments?
- Does your community encourage attractive land-efficient and cost-efficient traditional development patterns?
- Is personal income growth the most important economic indicator?
- Is your community attractive to and supportive of small businesses?
- Does your community have a strong technology infrastructure?
- Is your community planning for an efficient mass transit system?

8. Build Beautifully and Steward the Environment –

Buildings and architecture reflect a community's values. Growth, however, should be balanced with stewardship.

- Does your community have architectural and landscape design guidelines?
- Are architects and artists involved in community decision-making?
- Are new public buildings in your community designed to the highest standard?
- Does your community have a viewshed management plan for its roadways?
- Does your community have one place that is recognized as its heart?
- Does your community promote public art?
- Does your community have highly visible green space?
- Does your community require protection of environmentally sensitive areas?
- Does your community encourage alternative transportation such as walking and bicycling?
- Does your community actively integrate a recycling program into the daily activities of its citizens and businesses?
- Does your community have an abundance of parks of all types?

- Does your community adequately protect water quality?
- Does your community have a brownfields clean-up program?
- Does your community regulate vehicle emissions?

9. Recruit, Retain, and Generate Wealth – Cities must work to attract new businesses and new residents while nurturing existing ones.

- Does your community rely primarily on innovation and creativity for economic growth?
- Is your community's business climate known for its openness, flexibility, and vitality?
- Is your community's economic infrastructure, including digital infrastructure, up to date?
- Does your community place great value on helping local business grow?
- Does your community engage in active business recruitment worldwide?

10. Overcome Obstacles – Seek out solutions from unexpected places or from others who are doing it well. Successful projects in other cities can often be replicated.

- Does your community invite outside experts to share new ideas?
- Do your leaders visit other communities that have managed to replicate successful ideas?
- Does your community have a vision for self-improvement?
- Does your community think outside the box?
- Is your community afraid of failure, or success?

11. Rethink Boundaries – Cities must expand their boundaries by seeking partnerships with businesses, surrounding communities, and other local governments.

- Does your community create economies of scale by partnering with other communities and agencies?
- Does your community consider the impact of local decisions on surrounding communities?
- Does your business community welcome new businesses—even if they may be seen as competitors?

12. Buy Locally, Sell Globally – Cities must connect their social and economic well-being to the global marketplace and identify opportunities beyond their local footprints. Using and allocating local resources—human, economic, or material—to tap into the world at large brings new wealth and knowledge into the local community.

- Does your city have a business incubator program?
- Does your city effectively market itself and its businesses on the Internet?
- Does your community provide educational training for entrepreneurs to market their products globally?
- Is your community an active participant in the New Economy?
- What percentage of your local economy is a direct result of marketing via the Internet?
- Does the world knock at your door because of the quality of life, leadership, or products provided?
- Does your community or its citizenry receive regional, national, or global media coverage because of its accomplishments?